# Gay First Times
## 10 Gay Men Share
## Their First Time with a Man

I0421273

## Clark Wilder

# Table of Contents

# Part I

# Get Ready

# Introduction

*Gay First Times* is a collection of 10 men detailing their first time sexual experiences with a man. The accounts of their first sexual experience with another man are hot, tantalizing, with nothing being held back. Asked by author Clark Wilder to provide as much detail as possible, they disclosed every sexy detail in their recounts of these intensely intimate experiences.

You are about to uncover sexy guy on guy stories:

Derek's First Time

RV Games with Jason

Movie Night with Nate

Hot Soccer Players

Tyler in the Dorm

Craig's Massage

Alex in Amsterdam

Dressing Room with Giovanni

College Nights

Dominic at My Beach House

In *Gay First Times*, you will hear from real men and read about their real first time gay experience stories. Exciting, explicit, and tempting, this book is sure to please and is refreshingly real!

# Chapter One

## Craig's Massage

I had been friends with Craig since junior high. We were both still seniors in high school when we had our first sexual experience together. He identified as gay and I identified as straight at the time.

I remember him asking me if I would ever hook up with a guy. I said "I don't think I could ever be attracted to a guy." I'm pretty sure Craig saw it as a challenge that I told him I wasn't into guys.

Craig was tall and bulked up in all the right places with tanned skin and dark hair. He carried himself as if he knew he was hot.

One day he asked me if I trusted my body. I asked him what he meant. He asked "I mean do you trust what your body tells you?" He said that I had formed an opinion from thoughts in my head that I couldn't be with a guy and that even though my mind was telling me one thing my body might tell me something different. He asked me, "If your body told you something different would you trust your body?"

I told him that I wasn't sure and he asked me if I was willing to try. He asked "Are you willing to give your body a chance to tell you what your mind might not yet know?" I said that I didn't know but maybe.

He took me to another room in his house. There was a massage table in his parents' spare bedroom with a bed sheet draped over. He asked me if I had ever had a massage. I replied "Yes" and he told me "Good, so you will be comfortable undressing for a massage." I smiled and told him to leave while I undressed and got on the table. I made sure to place the sheet over my entire body.

I remember feeling scared and I didn't know what to expect. I loved massage and I was tight from all the sports I played but I found myself more excited than I was just going to the spa. I knew it was because his hands would be on me and that feeling shocked me and made me so nervous.

He knocked gently, asked if I was ready, and I told him he could come in.

He told me "You have complete control. You can stop anything that happens at any moment. Feel free to tell me where you want massaged and where you don't."

I was lying face down on the table with my face in the cushioned cut out. I peeked with one eye and saw Craig had no shirt on. I smiled but he didn't see me. I remember shaking a bit in anticipation.

He had a bottle of massage oil on the dresser next to the table. I heard him open it up to release some into his hands.

He began massaging my neck and shoulders firmly.

He said "I am going to use my hands and some light massage oil and will be touching your skin." He asked me if I was okay with that. I replied "Yes."

He told me he was going to uncover my back. I swallowed hard and answered "Yeah that's cool."

He drew the sheet back slowly, exposing my back. He was careful not to uncover my underwear still hidden under the sheet. As he began to rub me down, he told me I was holding a lot of stress and tension in my shoulders and back.

I heard his rub her palms together to warm the oil, and he spread the warmed oil across my skin. Then he slid his thumbs down along my back muscles playing across my warmed skin. Gradually, I started to relax under his hands.

He let his fingertips brush along my sides as he worked down my arms by my ribcage. I stiffened a bit but I didn't say a word and at that moment I knew I was getting turned on. He worked down to the narrowing of my waist, letting his fingertips play across the small of my back, dipping just under the edge of the sheet to lightly brush the edge of my underwear. He quickly came back up to the top of my back and massaged.

When he gets back down to the small of my back, I am ready for him to go down further. At that point, he transitioned his hands to the sheet and stroked firmly down the outside of my thighs. His hands continue their transit up the back of my thighs and smoothly over the sheet and swell of my ass. As his hands approached the edge of the sheet, he slipped his fingertips under the sheet edge and played them across the top of my underwear.

I swear I thought I would have told him to stop but I couldn't. I was too excited and too aroused to make him stop. I remember wondering if I was gay and getting tense at certain points but his touch was so disarming, relaxing, and too arousing.

He continued rubbing my ass with his hands with the sheet still on my lower half. His open palms caressed my thighs and I relaxed into the sensation. Then, he continued the caress down the length of my firm, long legs.

"May I lift the sheet to work on your legs?" he asked.
I remember nodding yes and not being able to speak.

He lifted the bottom of the sheet up and uncovered my feet, calves, and massaged them firmly as he worked his way up. I remember he told me that my legs were strong and it felt so good hearing that from him. As he oiled his hands, stroked and caressed, he worked the sheet up to my thighs, firmly massaging their backs and sides but allowing his fingertips to lightly caress the sensitive skin of my inner thighs. My legs are still close together and while I'm relaxing, I still held myself tightly. Slowly, the sheet is just barely covering my underwear. He said, "I'd like to move the sheet up higher now, is that okay?"

"Yes," I said.

He lets his hands roam freely over me, down my sides, to my waist, across my ass, down my thighs, back up into my inner thighs. My thighs part incrementally with each pass and he begins rubbing my between my thighs and into my groin. I'm sure he notices that my ass is up in the air a bit because of my erection now that he is so close to me. He rubs gently, then proceeds to rub more firmly. I can hear him breathing hard.

"It's time to turn over onto your back now" he says.

I turn over without hesitation and I allow the sheet to slip off onto the floor. My heart is racing now. I'm on my back wearing only underwear.

He begins to massage my upper pectoral muscles and down my stomach. He caresses my chest and then down my rib cage. Massaging my stomach, he works the tension out of me while massaging my hips and fronts of my thighs. He follows the ridge of my hips into the tight groin tendons, and my thighs part giving him more access.

"I'd like to remove these now," he says.

I lift my hips in response without a word or hesitation.

He slips the underwear down quickly but gently. He resumes massaging the muscles of my upper thighs.

As he works the rest of the stress and tension out of my body, he leans over and breathes a warm breath across my nipple and lets his breath out shakily.

"Should I continue?" he asks. I can't keep up the pretense of calm control anymore. I know he can feel the desire in my body.

"Yes," I whisper.

He moves to stand at the head of the table and drops down so his mouth is right by my ear. "I want to taste you now."

I bite my bottom lip and breathe my consent.

He lightly licks the curve of my ear and then draws my earlobe between his teeth, grazing it gently. I shiver and the goose bumps rise down my arms and chest. He kisses and licks around my nipple. He sucks the sensitive flesh and flicks the tip of his tongue rapidly over the peak until I moan. He rolls the other nipple between his thumb and forefinger and squeezes gently. My fingers tangle in his hair as I pull him against me.

He slips his hand down and caresses my inner thigh firmly. I can feel the damp heat radiating from my core. He kisses his way down to my stomach as his hand moves up. He pauses and I'm silent until finally I whisper, "Yes"... "Yes".

He slips his fingers into my heated oiled up cock and rubs me until I'm weak from pleasure. My orgasm pumped warm cum into his hand and he smiled with satisfaction in his eyes. I'll never forget it.

# Chapter Two

## RV Games with Jason

The first experience I had with a boy...I was in my teens. I'm 19 now. The guy that I was friends with was Jason. We were friends for a very long time. At that time, my family had an RV. When my friends would come over we would all hang out in the RV.

One night, Jason was drinking while we were hanging out. He was drunk and we were playing video games. I was sober though. We got bored at one point and he asked me to kiss him. I was like "Whoa, no bro I can't I'm not like that bro, but if you are that's cool... but I can't."

After that night, he kept on about it. For the next month or so he kept asking me almost every time we hung out if I would kiss him. Every time I would tell him no. But I hadn't even kissed a girl before. Finally, I was like okay and I thought what the hell let's just do it. We went into the RV and I let him kiss me. I ended up kissing him back and we made out for a good while. I felt that spark. Something went off and I knew there was something special about him after that kiss.

For weeks we would make out every time we saw each other. But being the bold and brazen guy that Jason was, one day he asked if he could have sex with me. I had already felt so comfortable with him and my hormones were raging by this point. I said yes.

I remember him telling me "I promise, no matter what happens, we will never regret this." I think he knew how much I liked him more than I even knew myself. His words were reassurance enough for me to give myself fully to him sexually.

In a moment, I found myself breathless and straining to get closer to Jason's solid warmth. He had pulled down his pants by now and revealed his hard dick. He placed his body against me while were still standing and started licking from my neck to my ear and kissing my lips. Jason sat down at the edge of the bed in the RV and stroked his dick a few times for me to watch. Then asked me to go down. I got down on my knees and opened my mouth. He guided himself into my salivating mouth. I began licking and sucking and the more I did the more I wanted him on top of me and inside of me. I knew what I wanted by that point.

Luckily, he hadn't came yet (I may not have known exactly how to make him cum with my mouth at that time). I got up and turned around for him to put my ass on his face. I bent over a little bit for him to see. He moaned and rubbed and opened my ass. He liked what he saw. He revealed to me a condom he had stolen from his older brother. I was shocked but pleased because I knew now he was ready to Fuck me.

He opened the condom like a pro. I turned around to watch while he put it on his throbbing dick. I laid down onto the mattress when he finished putting it on and laid flat on my back on the mattress. He got on top and pulled a bottle of what I now know was lube and rubbed it all over his dick. I was nervous...very nervous, but he looked so sure of himself and knew what he wanted. He slowly probed his dick into me while he kissed me deeply. I'll never forget his sex and the way he sounded when he came inside of me. It was like nothing I had ever experience in my life.

We were best friends for three years and romantically involved for another two years. For those two years we were never apart. He ended up moving to Maine but I never forgot about him. He recently got in touch with me through social media and I'm trying to save up money to go see him soon.

# Chapter Three

## Movie Night with Nate

It was on Halloween weekend a couple of years ago, and my best friend Nate and I were on the couch watching a horror movie marathon. By the time we were starting the third movie, it was getting late and cold in my apartment.  Nate grabbed a big blanket that I kept next to the couch and threw it over both of us. He was sitting in the corner of the couch, so I snuggled back against him and then we pulled the blanket over and around both of us.

About half way through the movie, I got up to go use the restroom (we were drinking martinis). When I got back, I pulled the blanket off Nate and then sat back down between and leaned against his shoulder. He shook the blanket out and the pulled it back over us and then pulled his hands back inside the blanket and went to rest one of them on my thigh. When he did this, he not only pulled his hands inside the blanket, but also pulled them inside my shorts. I jolted.  It wouldn't have been such a big deal, but I was in my boxer shorts, so his cold hands went right inside almost grazing the shaft of my penis. Didn't expect that.

"What was that Nate?" I asked.

"I didn't mean to, perv, I was just trying to get my arms back under the blanket," he said in her defense.  And while doing so, Nate joked and squeezed my thigh really hard, saying "Oh, baby, baby."

We laughed and then began to watch the movie again. About twenty minutes later, Nate took a drink of his drink, and then placed his hands back under the blanket. He had been doing this the entire time during the movie, but this time it was different. When he put his hands back under the blanket, he also put them high up on my thigh again, but this time very slowly almost caressing me. I looked over at him, but he was looking down with his eyes closed. I froze, but didn't stop him. His hands continued to lightly brush my skin and walk their way up to my thigh. What was he doing? Was my best friend really going to feel me up for real? The thought of it had my mind racing and my heart pounding. I wondered for a second if I should stop him but I didn't.

He was massaging up close to my inner thigh almost to my groin. His hand felt warm and sensual. My dick reacted almost instantly and I immediately became partially erect. He gently squeezed my leg and let his fingers graze my groin area. I pushed my shoulder into him, and that was all he needed to be encouraged. His left hand now came in as well and started its way up my stomach and up to my chest.

We were still under the blanket. It felt so good having his warm hands massaging me. I could feel myself getting turned on even more. He must have been thinking about this since he playfully grabbed my thigh earlier. I had no idea he wanted this, but I was loving it.

The better he made me feel, the more I pushed my body into him. I was getting very hard and was wondering if he was as well. I was being taken over by sexual desire.

With that, I slid my right hand down the waistband of my boxers. Yep, I was already hard as Fuck. I started stroking myself slowly knowing that he could feel my actions. Just then, Nate leaned toward my ear and whispered with his hot sexy voice, "Do it, Jake."

That was all I needed to hear. I played with myself while leaning against his body and it felt amazing. Having Nate playing with my nipples, rubbing all over my chest and stomach, massaging my groin, and encouraging me to get myself off was unbelievably erotic. I was feverishly stroking my dick. My breathing became shorter and erratic. I was getting close. Nate could tell and began squeezing my nipples harder. "Yes. Do it. Cum for me."

His breath was so hot and sexy in my ear. My body was so hot and aching with desire. I wanted to cum for him. I wanted to cum for another guy. "Yes, I'm cumming!" I said. My body shook although I tried so hard to stay still. I closed my eyes at the peak of my orgasm.  It felt so sensual as Nate held me tight until my orgasm subsided.

A couple of minutes later, I pulled my hand out of my now wet boxers and brought it up to my lap. Nate brought his hand down to reach mine. He grabbed my hand and then brought it up to the top of the blanket until just my finger was poking out. Next thing I knew I felt a warm sensual feeling on my finger. Nate had taken my hand into his mouth and was sucking on it. He licked it clean and then brought my hand back down to my lap where we held hands for the rest of the movie.

# Chapter Four

# Hot Soccer Players

I felt like we had the world's hottest guy on our soccer team. He had the perfect body for me, and a lot of times I would catch myself staring at him on the field, quick to turn away if he saw me. Ever since the first time I saw him, I had fantasized about him.

Watching him was exactly what I was doing this early one Wednesday morning. We planned to travel with the team to the Cup tournament in Miami and we were about to leave soon.

Once at the Cup site we set up our sleeping gear in the classroom we had been allocated. My heart skipped a beat when Anthony (the guy I crushed on) threw his mattress next to mine. I wondered why he settled there and not in one of the corners far away, as usual. We were friendly with each other during practice but outside of soccer we didn't hang out.

We had traveled far to get to the Cup. It was already late when we had settled in, and with a game the next day, we went to bed early. Just before I was about to fall asleep, I felt Anthony's fingers gently stroking me along my arm. It only lasted a few seconds and he stopped just as quickly as he started. I could not be absolutely certain that he meant to touch me. Despite my doubts I shivered and strangely wanted him to continue, but he didn't.

The next day was the first game of the tournament. I didn't think about Anthony's caress the previous night, until he caught my eye during breakfast. He smiled at me. All morning my mind was preoccupied with him.

Later that day, I asked him to take a walk with me. After walking for a while I remember stopping to sit on a bench. We sat next to each other in silence for a moment and looked at the starry sky. At least he did. I was just too focused on his right leg touching mine.

We got up and started walking again. We talked about the game and other things. We crossed an open area and reached the start of a path. I turned around to start going back, but stopped suddenly at the entrance to the path.

"What is it, Anthony?" I asked, and turned back to him. He said nothing and only looked at me. I remember getting caught up in his eyes. My heart raced. He took a step closer to me and he let the back of his hand caress my cheek. I held my breath as his face approached mine. I could feel his breath on my lips, and now I would finally get to feel his lips against mine. Then his cell phone rang.

"Damn," he mumbled and he went ahead and answered it.

Days passed during the tournament. We tried to get a moment alone, but there was always someone who ruined it for us. I saw how frustrated Anthony became. Matches went well for us. On Saturday we played in the semifinals, unfortunately losing 2-1 after extra time. So on Monday we played for third place, and won 2-0. Afterwards, came all the euphoria of victory and everyone congratulated each other with handshakes and hugs. I held Anthony closely for a long moment as my hands explored his lower back. Before he released me, he let his lips press into my cheek and I shivered.

The following day we were headed home. I was really irritated because Anthony and I still had not managed to be alone. When we arrived home, it was inevitable, that all would surely be back to normal but I wanted whatever was happening between us to continue.

We hadn't seen each other for a few weeks, besides with the team, but he continued to smile and stare at me.

After one workout, I decided to take a shower because I planned to visit some guy friends afterwards. Expecting to have the dressing room all to myself, I was shocked when Anthony followed me into the showers.

"Well, why are you showering here, when usually you're not?" he asked me.

I said "No, I usually don't. But today I am visiting some friends, so I thought it was better that I shower here and then go there straight away," "You then, why are you also here?"

"Ha-ha," laughed Anthony. "For the same reason, actually." We laughed.  He smiled and stepped out of his clothes trying to look away as I got out of my clothes.

We stepped into the shower and I couldn't take my eyes off his tall lean smooth body. When I looked up at him, I blushed, realizing that he knew I was eying him. He looked at me the same way that he had on the tournament trip, when we almost kissed.

He took a cautious step toward me. We stood facing each other, with almost no space separating our bodies. Anthony extended his hands and placed them on top of my shoulders. He then pulled me close and let his lips meet mine. I exploded inside. I couldn't believe this was happening...finally.

I pulled him toward me while we kissed. I got to feel his naked body next to mine. His hands eagerly caressed my back and thighs and they made their way to my lower stomach. My hands massaged his body and quickly found his tight butt. He groaned as both my hands for the first time fondled his ass. In response he kissed me harder, and he forced me back against the wet shower wall.

His hands caressed my wet abs, and slid teasingly on close to the base of my cock. Suddenly, he reached down to my inner thighs and cupped my balls. His fingers slowly teased around my erect cock. When he finally grabbed my cock, I was fully hard.

He turned the shower off and said "Come on." That's when he pulled me away, threw our towels on the floor in the middle of the locker room and laid me down.

His lips met mine again. My hands slid further down and caressed his cock. He groaned and we rolled onto our sides. His hands went behind my back to pull me next to him. He grazed his lips over my neck and throat, and I could feel my body shaking. I moved my hand to his dick and gently stroked again, as he moaned. I knew it was his first time as well. I could tell by looking in his eyes. My touches became more forceful, and he moaned louder and louder, finally screaming in pleasure. I could not believe I was actually doing this with him...I was jerking off the guy I had stared at and fantasized about for so long.

Seeing him pleasured made me very hard, and I stopped when he was finished cumming. I saw in his eyes what he was about to do. He kissed my neck, and I leaned my head back. His kisses walked further down my body. He took his time to kiss my abs, my thighs, before his lips found their way to my swollen cock. He kissed and licked my cock as I moaned with excitement. He finally let his tongue sweep across my shaft. I moaned and began to thrust my hips up to his face. His tongue probed and circled my cock slowly. He grabbed the base of my cock with his hand

and began swallowing and sucking my cock. I remember it was not long before I tensed my entire body and screamed while I came. Then my body went limp, in total relaxation, as he opened his eyes and smiled at me.

I felt his hands again on my stomach. He smiled happily and crawled back up to me. His fingers stroked softly over my cheek and he kissed me.

"I love you," he whispered.

# Chapter Five

## Tyler in the Dorm

Tyler and I shared a dorm room in college. One night, we were partying and by the time we got to the second party we were already pretty intoxicated. It was around 1:30 AM and I was ready to go back to the dorms but Tyler said he heard the girl he was talking to would be at this house, so we went.

The house party was crowded. Tyler scanned the first room, and I moved toward the kitchen to find more alcohol. In the kitchen there was a group of girls.

"So, how do you guys know each other?" one of the girls asked.

"We're roommates," Tyler answered, "this is my best friend!" He hugged me, letting his hands fall and rest on my ass.

The girls asked us back to their place, but we agreed we were tired and ready to go back to our dorm.

When we got in our room, we immediately started undressing like we normally would. Usually when Tyler is changing, I sneak a few glances at his body. That night I found myself staring.

His ass was bigger than mine, and I'd always wanted to feel it. It was round and perky and looked so sexy in and out of boxers. He was practically naked now, and I was too. I wanted to get closer to him.

I took my underwear off and didn't bother looking for a shirt or shorts to sleep in. My dick was slightly hard and I wanted him to see. Now, more than anything, I wanted Tyler to touch me. We had never been that drunk with each other and I had a feeling he landed his hand on my ass earlier on purpose. He had told me before that he was attracted to guys. I guess he felt comfortable telling me because he knew I identified as bisexual at the time.

He turned around so we were facing each other wearing nothing. I smiled at him.

"Why haven't we experimented?" he asked me, "We're buzzed...we like guys. Why shouldn't we mess around?" He said as he stared at my eyes.

I moved toward him. I let the alcohol take over and I said "I want to be inside of you." He pulled me closer and kissed me hard.

"I'm so horny," he moaned, "I want you so bad. Please Fuck me."

We moved to our sofa and I sat him down as I stood. I let my dick grind against his chest and graze his face as I gave him a lap dance. He moaned and slapped my ass leaving imprints.

"Sit on my face," he commanded. I positioned my ass over his face and spread my tight ass cheeks. His tongue probed my hole and I moaned as I felt it inside of me. Then he started to lick and tease, making me want him even more. I squeezed and played with my own nipples, watching him taste me.

After a minute, I got down on my knees as he sat on the sofa. I grabbed his dick and gave it a few strokes as I looked at him trying to see if he liked what I was doing to him. He closed his eyes and put his head back so I continued. I gave his dick a few more licks and began sucking like I had seen in porn before. His legs shook and I knew he was turned on. I sucked it the best that I could. It felt amazing having his hot cum squirt into my mouth. At first I held it in my mouth, until I remembered to swallow his sweet cum.

Just then, he picked me up and laid me down on the sofa face first on my stomach. He licked his fingers and started fingering me. With my ass in the air, he paused for a moment and got something which I quickly realized was a condom and lube. He placed it on himself while he fingered me slowly and licked all around my tight ass. He pulled his finger out slowly and thrust his hips toward me letting the tip of his dick probe slightly into me. Then he told me to relax as he kissed my back and luckily I did because he slid half way inside and started fucking me. When I heard him about to bust, I came harder than I ever had in my life. Afterwards, he licked the cum off my dick and sucked me until I couldn't take it anymore.

We were both more than ready to go to sleep. We ended up holding each other that night.

We said goodnight and I hoped we would do this again and we did....again, and again, and again.

# Chapter Six

## Derek's First Time

My first time was in high school. I was with someone that I had been friends with for a while. I remember he had a gorgeous movie star smile. He was tan with large pecs for his age and toned abs. His name was Trey.

I was still in the closet and I swore he was straight but you never know with people that young. I invited him to my house and we got in the hot tub and kind of got all wet and just relaxed. We ended up going back up into my room. We had gone in the hot tub in our underwear so everything was tight and wet and sticking to our bodies. So as he was drying off all I could do was stare at his dick because it was just bulging out...and he noticed.

He gave me a look that said "Do you like what you see?" At that point, I had never done anything with anyone let alone a guy. I wasn't sure what to do. But I had seen videos. So I got on my knees like I had seen in videos. I kind of stuck one hand up his briefs and one hand down and just pulled his dick out. I kept staring at it because it was something so new for me. All I did was put him in my mouth. I didn't quite know what I was doing but it felt right.

I sucked him for a little while, got up, held his jet black hair and kissed him. It felt right. I didn't know if I was gay before but it felt right and I felt like definitely I was into guys. We made out. He was a little hesitant about pleasuring me but he finally went down on me.

He got down on his knees. He undressed me and he put his mouth on me. He said my dick was nice which felt like a huge compliment. He sucked me until I came which only took a few minutes. The rest is history but I still get hot when I think about Trey.

# Chapter Seven

## Alex in Amsterdam

It's ridiculously hot where I live in Palms Springs and I can't even breathe. I don't have an AC in my house. It's 95 degrees right now here. I took three cold showers today and it's only the afternoon. I suppose the topic we're going to talk about today is pretty hot and steamy as well...my first gay sexual experience.

I remember this boy. He was beautiful. He was smart, sexy, and he was gay. This was back when I still lived in Amsterdam. Before meeting him, I had kissed boys before but nothing else. I always had girlfriends. I always told myself I was straight. I did fool around with boys but it never led anywhere. I was too young. I was too scared. It was kind of just like play to me.

Then, I met this boy and he was so hot and so beautiful. His name was Alex. He liked me and he was so bold when he would speak to me. With a hot accent, he said "I think you're hot and I think you like me too so I think we should get together." I said "You know I have girlfriend." He would be like "No, that's gonna change, there's no way you're going to have girlfriends."

At some point, he invites me to a party. We had a few drinks. The sexual tension was so insane I felt like I couldn't even sit next to him. I felt like, if I sat next to him he would hear my heart race because it was so fast and so loud.

I remember, one thing led to another, and we ended up in the back room of the house we were partying at and in the same bed. He kissed me and I kissed him back. I remember that was the first kiss where I felt like this might lead somewhere else. I thought we might end up doing something much more than kiss.

I was so nervous. I felt like I forgot how to kiss in that moment but I could tell he was so into it.

It felt like a movie, even though it sounds cliché. It felt like there were fireworks when we were kissing. I felt like I could breathe for the first time in my life. It was mind-blowing.

Before that night (the evening before I ended up in bed with him) I kind of figured something might happen because my girlfriend was away and I was able to do whatever I wanted to do. I was convinced even more when he told me "We're gonna do it. It's going to happen for you today." It was such a turn on how confident he was and how bold he was with me.

I wanted him so much but I remember worrying that I wouldn't know what to do. I thought "What do I do?" and "Where do I touch?" but the more we kissed the more I felt like I knew what to do. All my questions went away.

Alex had a lean, tan body. I gazed at it when we broke away from kissing. I took him in with my eyes. His body was so responsive to everything I did to him. He pushed my hand slowly with his hand until I could feel the tip of his hard dick. Right away, I began rubbing. I rubbed for a while. I didn't know if I was doing it right buy I assumed so since I got myself off all the time. We were kissing and breathing so hard almost in sync with each other.

He smelled like coconut tanning oil and I was hard by the time he was ready to touch me. I looked at his gorgeous face with excitement. There was nothing that could stop me from pleasing him.

I realized at that moment that I loved pleasing a man. I began stroking him faster and more firmly.

I was glad that I had played with myself so much alone because I knew I needed to play with him. We were both so turned on that it felt like it took no time for him to cum all over my hand. He kissed me and then opened his eyes and stared at me smiling.

Then, he turned me over with his toned arms, placed his hands under my ass, and grabbed it while he slid his tongue across my exposed hard dick and opened up jeans. He pulled my underwear down hard. It was then that he proceeded to spread my legs and please my balls and dick with his entire mouth. I had never felt such big warm lips on my body in my life. I was so turned on that I came within minutes. I remember feeling him breathe hard onto me when I was finished cumming. He laid his face on my lower stomach and massaged my body with his strong hands.

Alex's sex opened up my world. It was amazing and beautiful. The connection between us made me throw all of my questions out. I never went back to having sex with girls again. He didn't become my boyfriend because he knew I was moving to the states. But he opened me up to a new world and I'll never forget him. If he's reading this...I'd love to thank him for the exciting ride.

# Chapter Eight

## Dressing Room with Giovanni

I remember one day back in high school shopping with my friend Giovanni and leading him into a popular sporting goods store. We looked through clothes and, after finding a couple of cool jerseys to try on, we headed for the dressing rooms. The dressing rooms were really nice. Each had a solid door and a nice long bench, and were very private. Giovanni also noticed that no one else seemed to be around, and got to thinking... it would be so hot to mess around right in the dressing room! We had kissed before but nothing else and we wanted each other badly that day.

I entered a dressing room and tried on a shirt. Giovanni was waiting outside. I opened it to show him my shirt. My toned arms were exposed.  Giovanni's eyes widened and told me, "You're so hot."

I pulled him into the dressing room, shut the door and kissed Giovanni as I pushed him against the wall. His hands roamed over my body, up and down, everywhere, as he kissed me on the neck and shoulders. He told me how much he had wanted me, but I got scared and replied, "We can't. Not in here. Let's go home..."

Giovanni said no one would know what we were doing if we were quiet, which made us both laugh. Because we both knew that we were much too passionate for silent kissing let alone quiet lovemaking.

He kissed me again. After more kissing, Giovanni unbuttoned my pants and took my hand and put it inside his underwear so I could feel how hard I had made him. When I felt the throbbing cock between his legs, he groaned into our kiss. He knew I needed him.

I remember nervously looking around while I started moving my hand against Giovanni's hard cock. The feeling of my fingers touching Giovanni was incredible. I took my hand and pushed under my jeans, sliding my underwear to the side so Giovanni would touch me.

We both became even harder. It felt like we knew exactly what to do to each other in that moment. At first we each rubbed all around each other's cocks. Then we both started stroking one another. We kept as quiet as possible despite the fact that we were so hot for each other. Our hips were thrusting into each other's hands and our mouths were devouring each other's lips. Giovanni's free hand grabbed my ass and pulled it tighter toward him, and I knew I was going to explode shortly.

He stroked my cock harder and then started to quicken his rhythm, ordering me to "come with me." We both gasped for breath and kissed frantically, grinding into each other when we felt ourselves coming. Giovanni told me he was going to come when he and I felt the explosion hit.

After we came, we stood there for a minute, just holding each other as we tried to calm down. I whispered, "We gotta go" as I removed my hand from Giovanni and then kissed him deeply.

We straightened our clothes while listening whether the coast was clear. We zipped up, I changed back into my own shirt, and left the dressing room wondering if anyone had heard us.

# Chapter Nine

## College Nights

Adam was my boyfriend. We'd just started college. I had been with a few guys already but had never penetrated anyone and Adam was still a virgin. He hadn't even slept with a girl much less a guy. We were in love and he asked me to take his virginity. This is our story of our first sexual experience together.

I remember one night we had together after going to a basketball game. Stumbling back into his room, he turned to me and we kissed. He took hold of my shirt and unbuttoned it, pulling me with him as he backed towards the bed. He sat on the edge of the bed and ran his hands over my chest as I stood in front of him.

He smiled at that, then unbuttoned my pants and pulled them down. Reaching up and taking hold of my boxer briefs, he released my dick, before looking up again.

I remember we were both wearing sweatpants with boxers because it was easy to see our erections bulging out. He pulled his sweatpants down to reveal his thick hard dick. Then, I reached down and ran my fingers over the head of it. I let my own sweatpants fall to the floor and knelt in front of him.

Pushing his legs apart either side of me, I shuffled forwards on my knees and kissed his stomach. I turned my attention to his chest, and kissed both nipples, before starting to lick and suck one while I rubbed soft circles over the other with my fingers.

He let out a small moan and ran his fingers through my hair, clutching me to him.

Moving my head slightly, I kissed in the middle of his chest, and then slightly lower, and lower again. Kissing down his stomach, I pushed his boxers down kissing against the base of his cock. He lay back and raised his legs, allowing me to peel his boxers down his legs and off his feet, before he set his legs back down.

I leaned in and ran my tongue along his groove, rewarded by a moan from Adam. Holding the base of his cock with my fingers, I searched out the tip of his cock with my tongue, drawing another moan as I slowly ran my tongue up and down over it. I licked him soft and slow for a minute or so, before pulling him towards me and pressing my tongue hard against his cock, diving in with my mouth all the way open and sucking, and starting to speed up.

He let out a moan at that, he reached down to place a hand on my head and held me against his throbbing cock. I stroked his cock as I continued to lick and suck his engorged unit, and started to pump hard as I tongued him.

Moaning loudly, his hips writhed up and down against my tongue, and he shouted as his breathing quickened "God I'm gonna cum, Fuck me!"

I stood and slid my cock between his ass cheeks and he waited impatiently while I put a condom with lube on. He gasped as I plunged it in. Just two thrusts later I felt his walls contract and he squeezed his nipples as his back arched.

I continued to pump my cock into his tight ass, thrusting rhythmically as he moaned and gasped. He told me he was cumming and moaned loudly.

I pressed my hips slowly forward into Adam and resumed a slow rhythm while I came inside of him. His legs were so long wrapped around me. After we both came, he laid there, hand between his legs. I moved in to kiss him again while still inside of him.

# Chapter Ten

## Dominic at My Beach House

My first time with a boy was a bit unexpected. I had invited Dominic over for a weekend at the beach at my Dad's beach house.

We were walking along the beach just talking about sports, our girlfriends, and all that kind of stuff. We somehow ended up talking about guys that we knew that were gay. After hearing how open and free-thinking he was, I ended up admitting to him that I thought I was bisexual. To my surprise he said the same about himself.

We got back to the beach house, had dinner, and watched a movie. Somehow we ended up holding hands.

I had a double bed there so I knew we would be sleeping right next to each other. I knew something was going to happen since we both liked guys. I could feel the tension between us. We were nervous.

It was pitch black and we were close but not touching. I could feel his warm breath on me. I crossed my leg over his and he grabbed my hand above my head.
Our thighs were touching now.

All of a sudden I was kissing him! I sat on top of him with my semi-erection pressed against his thigh. I started grinding on his leg. I was already aroused and I'm sure he could feel it.

Our sudden make-out session slowed and I told him to take his shirt off. He did and I did the same. I took his nipple in one hand and stroked his already erect nipple. Guiding my other hand down his body, I pulled down his pajama shorts and found his dick. I rubbed around the tip of his dick in circles... a little bit harder and faster until he was breathing heavily against me. In the dark, I found his chest with my mouth and started licking and sucking his nipples.

He was moaning and pushing his hips up to me. I took this as a sign to stroke harder and faster. I knew how I like it and that's what I did to him using my whole hand to rub his cock to climax. I could feel his muscles tightening and then the best sound in the whole world....
Him cumming!

He wanted more. I could feel the throbbing between my legs. I wanted him so badly I nearly came then and there. But he had different ideas.

He started licking and teasing my rock hard nipples. He moaned into my chest.
My cock was on fire now. I wanted him and needed him.

Moving away from my chest, he licked his way down my body till he found my throbbing dick. We were both panting and now I was biting my pillow to stop from moaning too loud. Pulling down my underwear, he got straight into it, caressing my glistening erect cock. Then his wet thick tongue found cock and he licked up and down then began sucking like he had done this before but I knew he hadn't.  His hard pecs were rubbing on my legs and I was so horny.

That's when I exploded in his mouth! He ate me up as I ground my cock on his face. I was cumming all down his face...it was the most amazing feeling ever!

Our bodies collapsed and we knocked out.

# Conclusion

Thank you again for downloading this book.

If you want more check my books out on Amazon and like my page on Facebook.

Until next time...

-CLARK WILDER

Love what you read?

Like **Clark Wilder Book Club** on Facebook for more!

www.ingramcontent.com/pod-product-compliance
Lightning Source LLC
Chambersburg PA
CBHW060345290526
45791CB00004B/1540